ALEXANDER HAMILTON
ACTIVITY BOOK

George Toufexis

DOVER PUBLICATIONS
Garden City, New York

There are plenty of activities to keep you entertained in this fun and educational book about one of our Founding Fathers, Alexander Hamilton. As you learn interesting facts about the birth of our nation, you can wind your way around mazes that lead you to Revolutionary War sites, figure out secret codes that will inform you about everyday life in the colonial era, determine the changes in a variety of paired drawings that may look the same but are slightly different, and much more! If you want to check your answers, or need a bit of help with any of the puzzles, solutions start on page 42.

Bibliographical Note

Alexander Hamilton Activity Book is a new work,
first published by Dover Publications in 2017.

International Standard Book Number
ISBN-13: 978-0-486-81852-8
ISBN-10: 0-486-81852-7

Manufactured in the United States by LSC Communications Book LLC
81852704   2021
www.doverpublications.com

ALEXANDER HAMILTON

Of all the Founding Fathers of the United States of America, Alexander Hamilton overcame more hardships than most of them. Born in poverty on a tiny island in the Caribbean, he was abandoned by his father, lost his mother to yellow fever, and was orphaned by age 13. But despite these incredible setbacks, Alexander managed to get to the British colonies in North America, receive an education, and rise to become a colonel in the Continental Army and a hero of the Revolutionary War. During the war, he was made personal assistant to General George Washington. After Independence, for the next twenty years, Hamilton would work with Washington on the framing of the U.S. Constitution, and as Washington served as President of the new United States of America. With a keen mind for economics, Hamilton was the first Secretary of the Treasury. He is also known for being one of the signers of the Constitution, as well as the founder of the United States Coast Guard and *The New York Post* newspaper. Hamilton also established the first national bank in the United States.

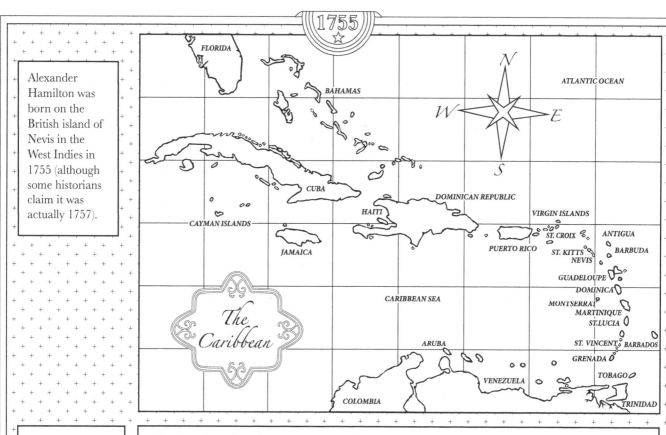

The Caribbean

Labels on map: FLORIDA, BAHAMAS, ATLANTIC OCEAN, CUBA, DOMINICAN REPUBLIC, HAITI, VIRGIN ISLANDS, ST. CROIX, ANTIGUA, CAYMAN ISLANDS, PUERTO RICO, ST. KITTS, BARBUDA, NEVIS, JAMAICA, GUADELOUPE, DOMINICA, CARIBBEAN SEA, MONTSERRAT, MARTINIQUE, ST. LUCIA, ARUBA, ST. VINCENT, BARBADOS, GRENADA, TOBAGO, VENEZUELA, COLOMBIA, TRINIDAD

Alexander Hamilton was born on the British island of Nevis in the West Indies in 1755 (although some historians claim it was actually 1757).

Find and circle these 12 island names in the puzzle to the right:

BAHAMAS

NEVIS

ANTIGUA

BARBUDA

CUBA

BARBADOS

TOBAGO

ARUBA

HAITI

JAMAICA

DOMINICA

GUADELOUPE

The words may appear forward, backward, vertically, or diagonally.

```
E S W C Q F A Y Q Q L T B Z T X Z O C U
F P I V C V D N D Z T S A Q D W B S R Z
V I U V N O S Y T S A N R I Q M W D T Q
X Z V O E V N U T I N M B C F V J D M P
X L B I L N M O F R G F U F E E R G B Y
N O P X Y E M O H M D U D C U B A Z J B
E I C A T M D C U K Z M A G L Q J A G N
L J L U O J I A P U W V K S I V M P W Y
A B L O F P S U U X M Y Q B A A O F C Y
H A A J I Q O E B G W X D I K V H K L
L K I T X G D L Z E H G A C F T Z E Q F
S Z I L H F A O K N R C A I C Z D W A O
J A J E O N B A C E I M R S Y U K A S L
H N L M M U R A B N D U D G X U O D J N
G P O N B H A K I K F O P V F Z M F A P
K C N D H M B M W U D O V S K T L A O B
U V F A M B O B A H A M A S O G A B O T
D H M C C D L J S P Y S J D G O T U K O
P B P X A P O H D R J E W N Y F R R T H
A T Z P S J L S B L G E F Q T W Y A H W
```

1768

Alexander Hamilton was orphaned as a young teen and worked hard at various jobs to support himself.

A	B	C	D	E	G	H	I	J	K	L	N	O	R	S	T	U	W

Young Alexander Hamilton had to dress for work. Find out the names for various colonial-era clothing he is wearing by using the alphabet code shapes above to write in the letters below.

British soldiers killed several colonists in an incident that became known as the "Boston Massacre." The soldiers were put on trial and local lawyer and future Founding Father John Adams defended them. This event only added more tension to the hostility between the Colonists and England.

There are several tools from the colonial era in this picture of a typical street in colonial Boston. Find and circle the seven tools shown on the left.

Sickle

Grain Shovel

Drawknife

Hatchet

Crow

Sugar Axe

Charcoal Iron

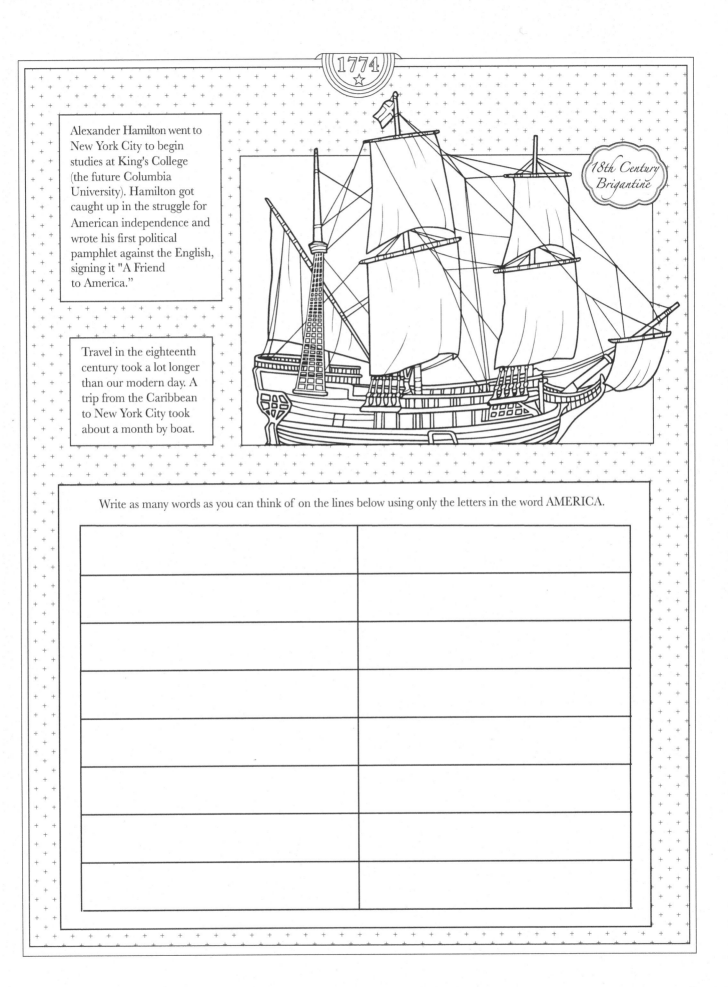

1774

Alexander Hamilton went to New York City to begin studies at King's College (the future Columbia University). Hamilton got caught up in the struggle for American independence and wrote his first political pamphlet against the English, signing it "A Friend to America."

Travel in the eighteenth century took a lot longer than our modern day. A trip from the Caribbean to New York City took about a month by boat.

18th Century Brigantine

Write as many words as you can think of on the lines below using only the letters in the word AMERICA.

On April 19, 1775, the first shots of the American Revolution were fired at Lexington and Concord. Hamilton, eager to participate in the fight for independence, joined the New York State militia.

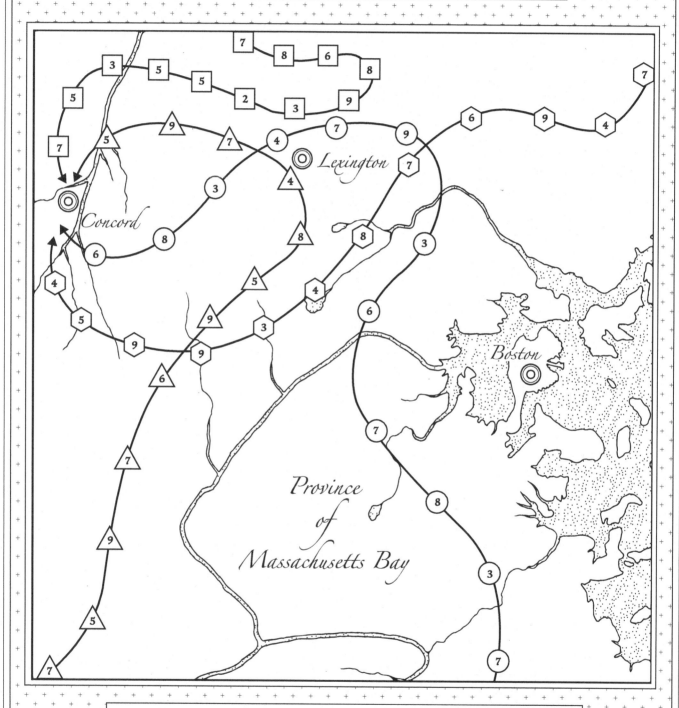

There are four different numbered paths leading to Concord. Only one path's numbers total 75. Draw a red line along that path.

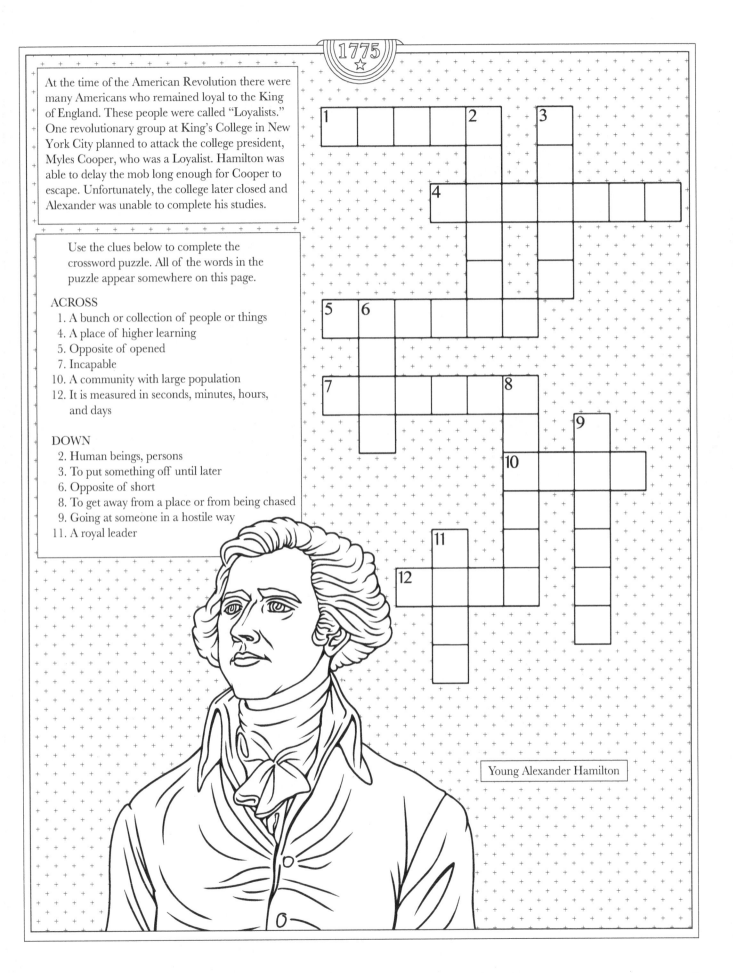

At the time of the American Revolution there were many Americans who remained loyal to the King of England. These people were called "Loyalists." One revolutionary group at King's College in New York City planned to attack the college president, Myles Cooper, who was a Loyalist. Hamilton was able to delay the mob long enough for Cooper to escape. Unfortunately, the college later closed and Alexander was unable to complete his studies.

Use the clues below to complete the crossword puzzle. All of the words in the puzzle appear somewhere on this page.

ACROSS
1. A bunch or collection of people or things
4. A place of higher learning
5. Opposite of opened
7. Incapable
10. A community with large population
12. It is measured in seconds, minutes, hours, and days

DOWN
2. Human beings, persons
3. To put something off until later
6. Opposite of short
8. To get away from a place or from being chased
9. Going at someone in a hostile way
11. A royal leader

Young Alexander Hamilton

7

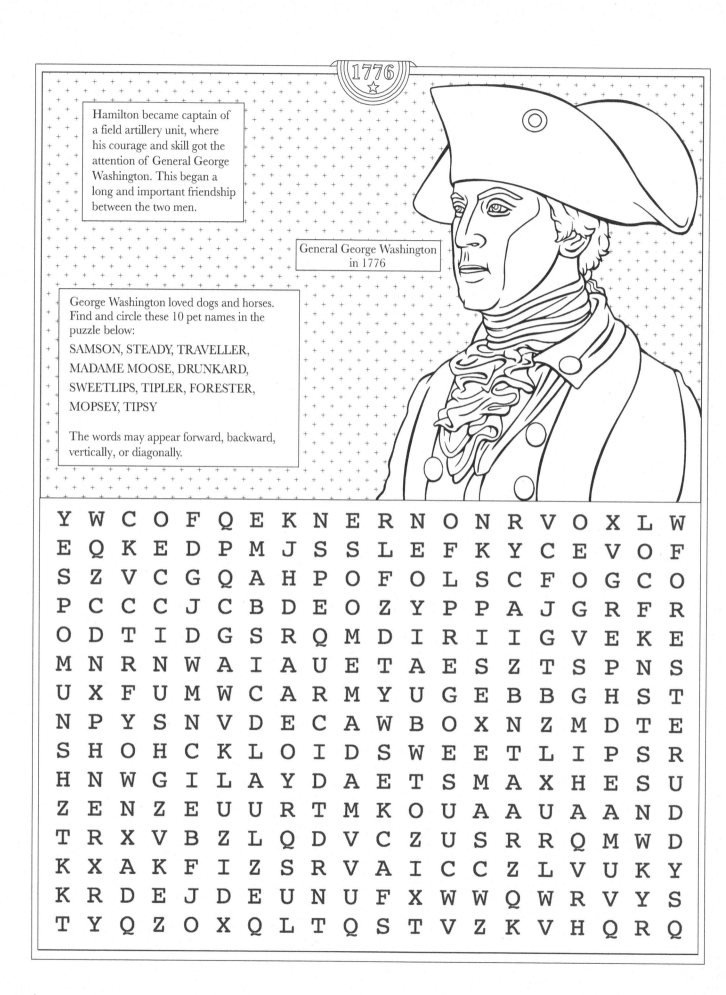

Hamilton became captain of a field artillery unit, where his courage and skill got the attention of General George Washington. This began a long and important friendship between the two men.

General George Washington in 1776

George Washington loved dogs and horses. Find and circle these 10 pet names in the puzzle below:

SAMSON, STEADY, TRAVELLER, MADAME MOOSE, DRUNKARD, SWEETLIPS, TIPLER, FORESTER, MOPSEY, TIPSY

The words may appear forward, backward, vertically, or diagonally.

```
Y W C O F Q E K N E R N O N R V O X L W
E Q K E D P M J S S L E F K Y C E V O F
S Z V C G Q A H P O F O L S C F O G C O
P C C C J C B D E O Z Y P P A J G R F R
O D T I D G S R Q M D I R I I G V E K E
M N R N W A I A U E T A E S Z T S P N S
U X F U M W C A R M Y U G E B B G H S T
N P Y S N V D E C A W B O X N Z M D T E
S H O H C K L O I D S W E E T L I P S R
H N W G I L A Y D A E T S M A X H E S U
Z E N Z E U U R T M K O U A A U A A N D
T R X V B Z L Q D V C Z U S R R Q M W D
K X A K F I Z S R V A I C C Z L V U K Y
K R D E J D E U N U F X W W Q W R V Y S
T Y Q Z O X Q L T Q S T V Z K V H Q R Q
```

On July 4, 1776, the Declaration of Independence was adopted by the Second Continental Congress and was read for all to hear on July 9th.

WE THE _ _O_ _ _ OF THE UNITED _T_ _ _ _, IN ORDER TO FORM A MORE _ _ _ _ _C_ UNION, ESTABLISH JUSTICE, INSURE DOMESTIC _ _ _Q_ _ _ _ _ _, PROVIDE FOR THE COMMON _ _F_ _ _ _, PROMOTE THE GENERAL _ _ _ _ _ _E, AND SECURE THE _L_ _ _ _ _ _ _ OF _ _ _ _ _T_ TO OURSELVES AND OUR _ _ _ _ _ _ _T_, DO ORDAIN AND ESTABLISH THIS _ _ _ _ _ _ _ _U_ _ _ FOR THE UNITED STATES OF _M_ _ _ _ _.

Above is the opening paragraph to the Declaration of Independence. Pick the correct words from the list below to finish each of the famous phrases, and write them in the blank spaces.

PERFECT

DEFENSE

STATES

BLESSINGS

AMERICA

TRANQUILITY

CONSTITUTION

WELFARE

PEOPLE

LIBERTY

POSTERITY

Color this historical flag with red and white stripes and gold stars on a blue background.

Color this U.S. Navy jack flag with red and white stripes; color the snake with light brown and gold.

DON'T TREAD ON ME

9

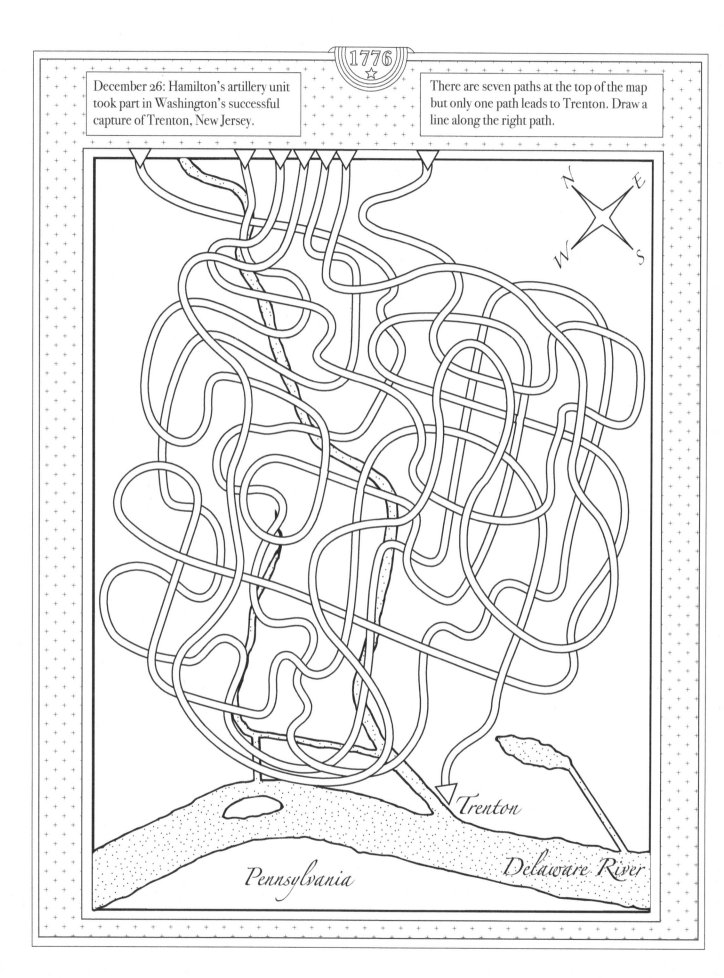

December 26: Hamilton's artillery unit took part in Washington's successful capture of Trenton, New Jersey.

There are seven paths at the top of the map but only one path leads to Trenton. Draw a line along the right path.

1776

Trenton

Pennsylvania

Delaware River

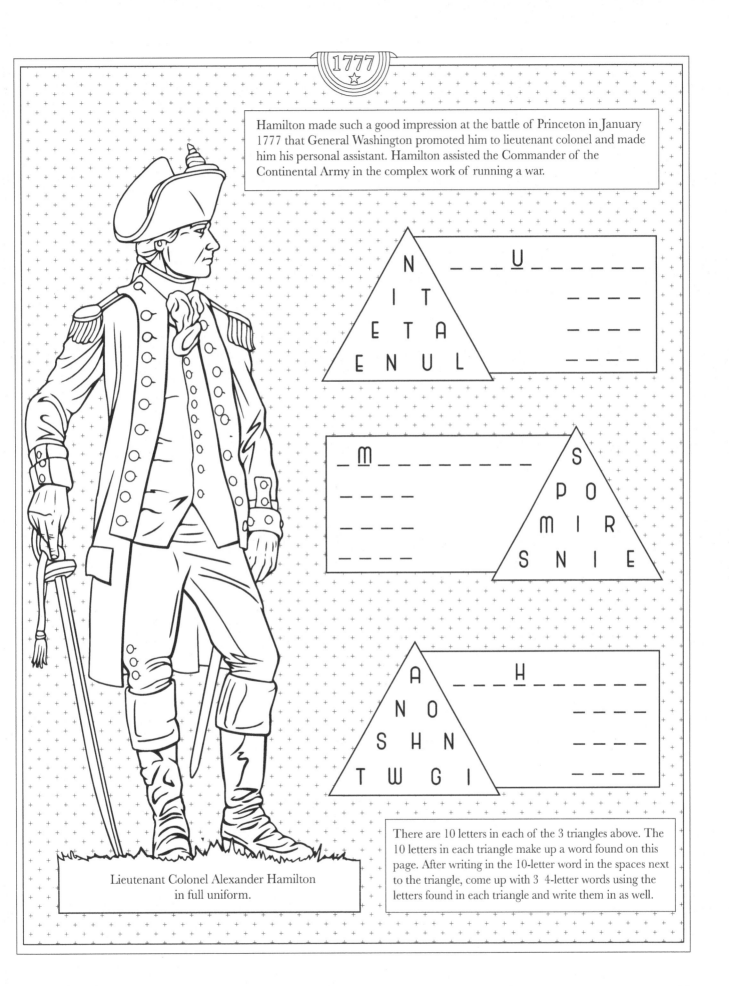

Hamilton made such a good impression at the battle of Princeton in January 1777 that General Washington promoted him to lieutenant colonel and made him his personal assistant. Hamilton assisted the Commander of the Continental Army in the complex work of running a war.

N
I T
E T A
E N U L

_ _ _ _ U _ _ _ _ _
_ _ _ _
_ _ _ _
_ _ _ _

_ m _ _ _ _ _ _ _ _
_ _ _ _
_ _ _ _
_ _ _ _

S
P O
M I R
S N I E

A
N O
S H N
T W G I

_ _ _ H _ _
_ _ _ _
_ _ _ _
_ _ _ _

Lieutenant Colonel Alexander Hamilton
in full uniform.

There are 10 letters in each of the 3 triangles above. The 10 letters in each triangle make up a word found on this page. After writing in the 10-letter word in the spaces next to the triangle, come up with 3 4-letter words using the letters found in each triangle and write them in as well.

11

Hamilton was almost killed in the battle of Monmouth. He was thrown from his horse but luckily survived without serious injury.

Draw the galloping horse on the grid below.

Hamilton didn't approve of slavery and wrote a letter to the Continental Congress with an idea of asking slaves to join the Continental Army, offering them freedom in exchange for their service.

Quill pens were made of goose, swan, or turkey feathers. There are nine feathers drawn on this page; circle the only two that are identical.

Alexander Hamilton and Elizabeth Schuyler (daughter of the wealthy General Philip Schuyler) fell deeply in love and were married just before Christmas.

The two fans on this page look identical but they are not. Draw a circle around each of the 10 differences.

Elizabeth Schuyler

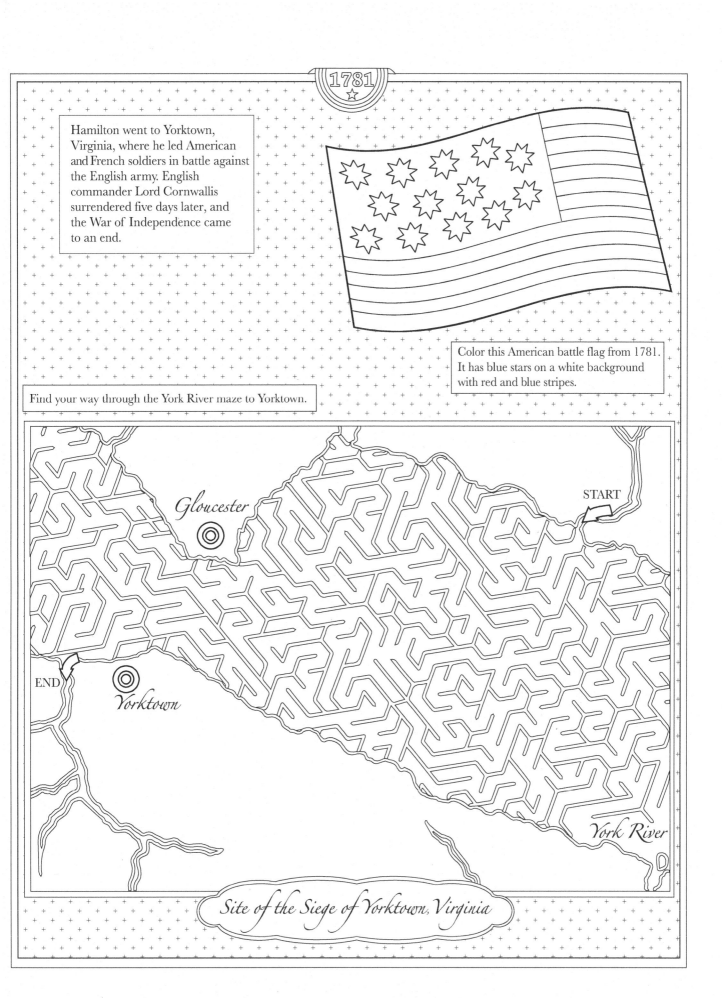

1781

Hamilton went to Yorktown, Virginia, where he led American and French soldiers in battle against the English army. English commander Lord Cornwallis surrendered five days later, and the War of Independence came to an end.

Color this American battle flag from 1781. It has blue stars on a white background with red and blue stripes.

Find your way through the York River maze to Yorktown.

START

Gloucester

END

Yorktown

York River

Site of the Siege of Yorktown, Virginia

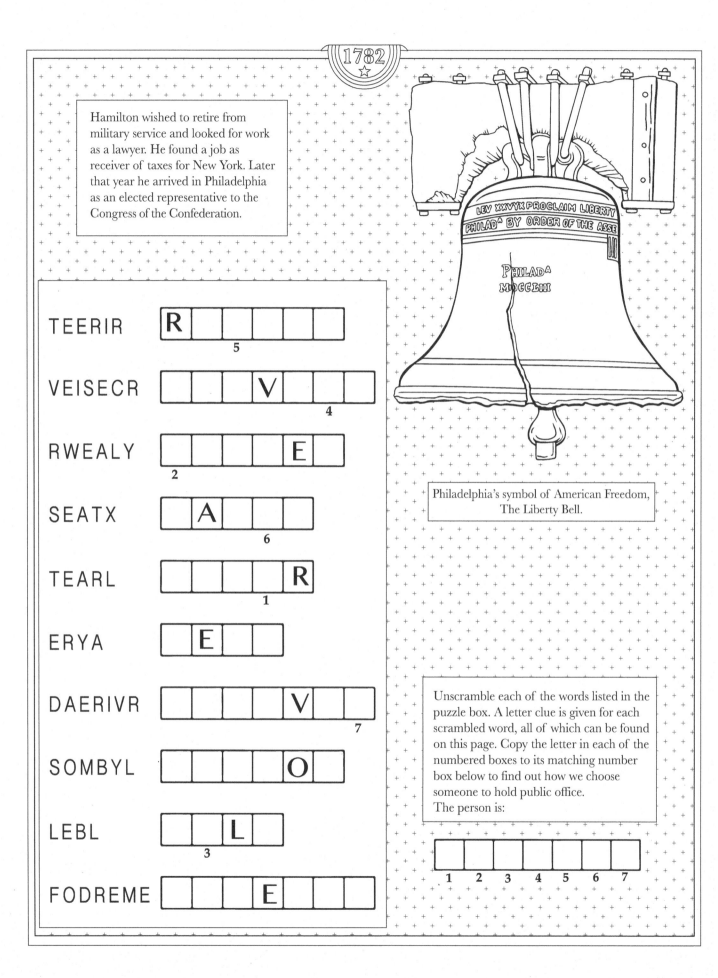

Hamilton wished to retire from military service and looked for work as a lawyer. He found a job as receiver of taxes for New York. Later that year he arrived in Philadelphia as an elected representative to the Congress of the Confederation.

LEV XXVYX PROCLAIM LIBERTY
PHILAD^ BY ORDER OF THE ASSE
PHILAD^
MDCCLIII

Philadelphia's symbol of American Freedom, The Liberty Bell.

TEERIR R [ ][ ][ ][ ]
               5

VEISECR [ ][ ][ ]V[ ][ ]
                   4

RWEALY [ ][ ][ ][ ]E[ ]
         2

SEATX [ ]A[ ][ ][ ]
             6

TEARL [ ][ ][ ][ ]R
           1

ERYA [ ]E[ ][ ]

DAERIVR [ ][ ][ ][ ][ ]V[ ]
                       7

SOMBYL [ ][ ][ ][ ]O[ ]

LEBL [ ][ ]L[ ]
       3

FODREME [ ][ ][ ]E[ ][ ]

Unscramble each of the words listed in the puzzle box. A letter clue is given for each scrambled word, all of which can be found on this page. Copy the letter in each of the numbered boxes to its matching number box below to find out how we choose someone to hold public office.
The person is:

[ ][ ][ ][ ][ ][ ][ ]
 1 2 3 4 5 6 7

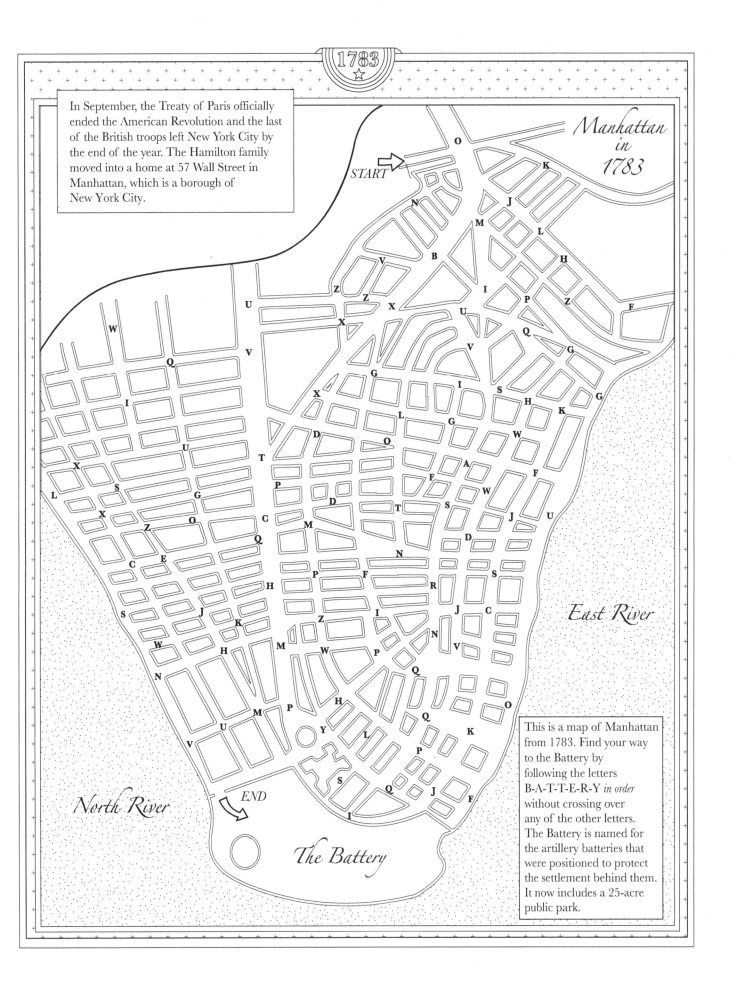

In September, the Treaty of Paris officially ended the American Revolution and the last of the British troops left New York City by the end of the year. The Hamilton family moved into a home at 57 Wall Street in Manhattan, which is a borough of New York City.

Manhattan in 1783

START

East River

North River

END

The Battery

This is a map of Manhattan from 1783. Find your way to the Battery by following the letters B-A-T-T-E-R-Y *in order* without crossing over any of the other letters. The Battery is named for the artillery batteries that were positioned to protect the settlement behind them. It now includes a 25-acre public park.

The Bank of New York, which Hamilton had helped develop, opened for business.

After the Revolutionary War, the American people did not trust paper money, so they did business with coins of gold and silver.

Alexander Hamilton appears on the U.S. ten dollar bill. In the blank space below, design your own piece of paper money with Hamilton, or anyone else of your choice, pictured on it.

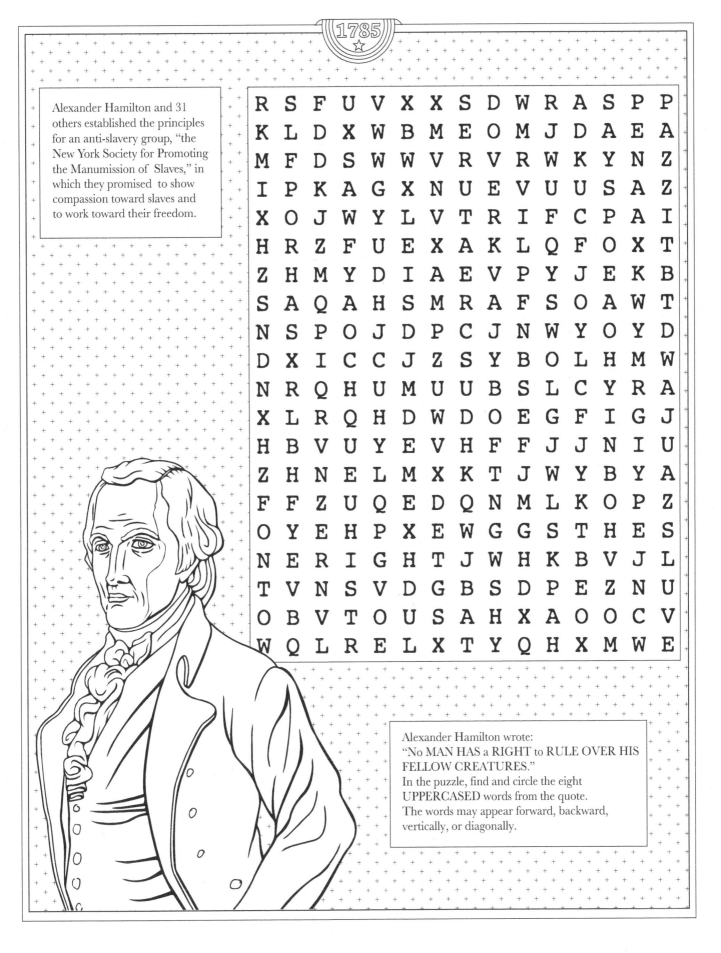

Alexander Hamilton and 31 others established the principles for an anti-slavery group, "the New York Society for Promoting the Manumission of Slaves," in which they promised to show compassion toward slaves and to work toward their freedom.

```
R S F U V X X S D W R A S P P
K L D X W B M E O M J D A E A
M F D S W W V R V R W K Y N Z
I P K A G X N U E V U U S A Z
X O J W Y L V T R I F C P A I
H R Z F U E X A K L Q F O X T
Z H M Y D I A E V P Y J E K B
S A Q A H S M R A F S O A W T
N S P O J D P C N W Y O Y D
D X I C C J Z S Y B O L H M W
N R Q H U M U U B S L C Y R A
X L R Q H D W D O E G F I G J
H B V U Y E V H F F J J N I U
Z H N E L M X K T J W Y B Y A
F F Z U Q E D Q N M L K O P Z
O Y E H P X E W G G S T H E S
N E R I G H T J W H K B V J L
T V N S V D G B S D P E Z N U
O B V T O U S A H X A O O C V
W Q L R E L X T Y Q H X M W E
```

Alexander Hamilton wrote:
"No MAN HAS a RIGHT to RULE OVER HIS FELLOW CREATURES."
In the puzzle, find and circle the eight UPPERCASED words from the quote.
The words may appear forward, backward, vertically, or diagonally.

Hamilton, representing the State of New York, attended a convention in Maryland to create rules and laws concerning business dealings between the new States of the Union. They produced a report that recommended plans to strengthen the general operation of the government of the United States.

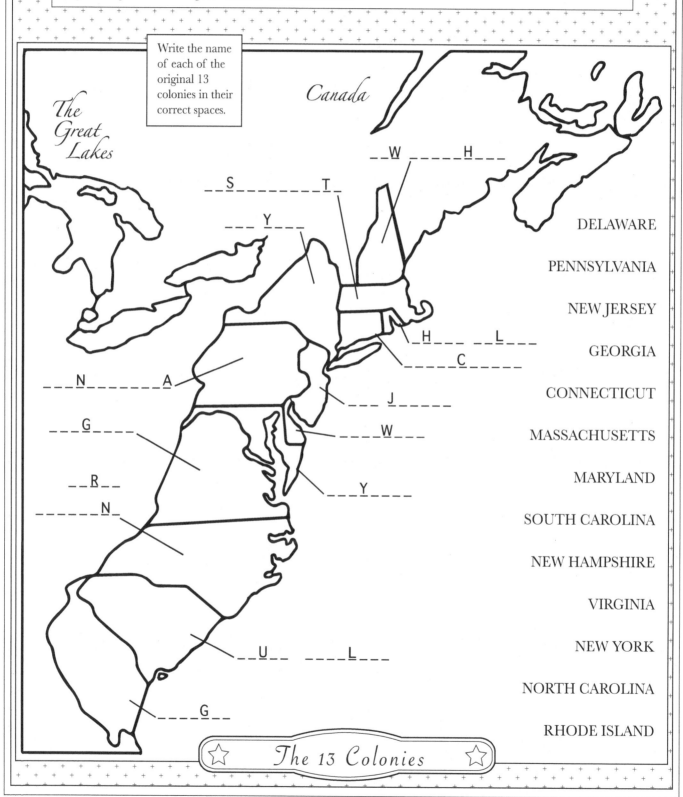

Write the name of each of the original 13 colonies in their correct spaces.

The Great Lakes

Canada

_ _ W _ _ _ _ _ H _ _ _

_ S _ _ _ _ _ _ _ _ T _ _ _

_ _ _ Y _ _ _

_ _ N _ _ _ _ _ A

_ _ G _ _ _ _

_ _ R _ _

_ _ _ _ _ N _ _ _

_ H _ _ _   _ _ L _ _ _ _
_ _ C _ _ _ _ _ _ _

_ _ _ J _ _ _ _ _

_ _ W _ _

_ _ _ Y _ _ _ _

_ U _ _   _ _ _ L _ _ _

_ _ _ _ G _ _

DELAWARE

PENNSYLVANIA

NEW JERSEY

GEORGIA

CONNECTICUT

MASSACHUSETTS

MARYLAND

SOUTH CAROLINA

NEW HAMPSHIRE

VIRGINIA

NEW YORK

NORTH CAROLINA

RHODE ISLAND

The 13 Colonies

The U.S. Constitutional Convention took place in Philadelphia. After several months, the delegates, including Hamilton, approved and signed the Constitution. It was sent to Congress, which in turn sent it to the States. Nine of the thirteen had to agree for the Constitution to be accepted.

George Washington

The list below includes the names of 20 of the 39 men who signed the U.S. Constitution. Find and circle the six names that don't belong.

George Washington

Benjamin Franklin

James Madison

Alexander Hamilton

Robert Morris

James Wilson

John F. Kennedy

John Rutledge

William Samuel Johnson

Albert Einstein

Richard Bassett

Richard Dobbs Spaight

Richard Nixon

Rufus King

Nathaniel Gorham

Long John Silver

Jonathan Dayton

Abraham Baldwin

Thomas Mifflin

George Clymer

Thomas FitzSimons

Abraham Lincoln

Jared Ingersoll

John Dickinson

Franklin Delano Roosevelt

John Blair

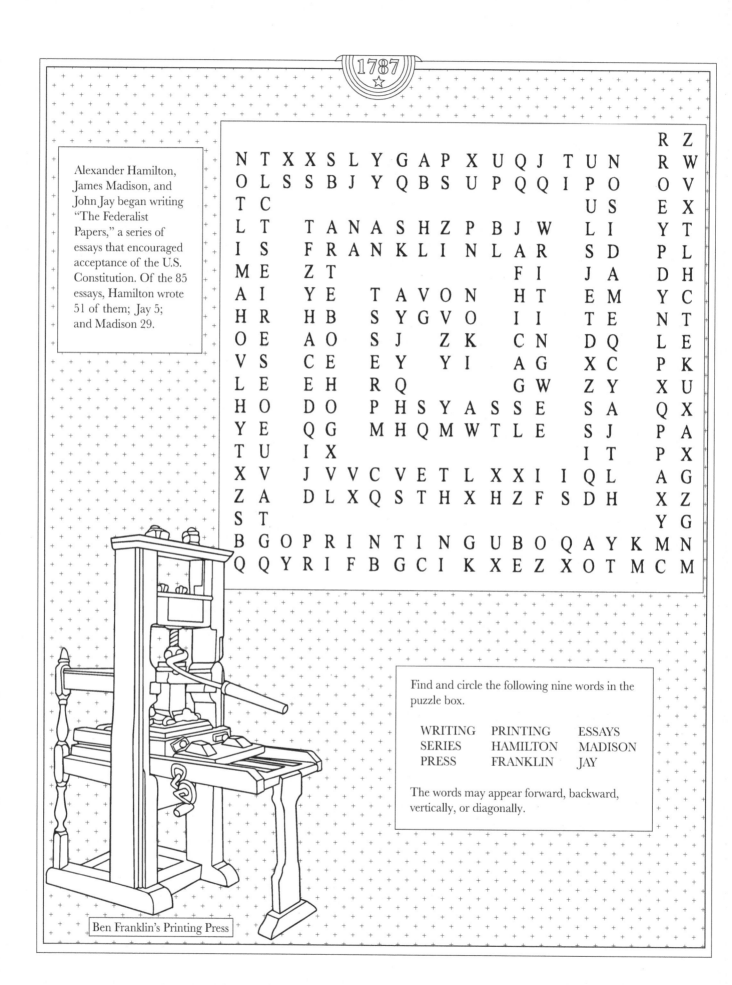

1787

Alexander Hamilton, James Madison, and John Jay began writing "The Federalist Papers," a series of essays that encouraged acceptance of the U.S. Constitution. Of the 85 essays, Hamilton wrote 51 of them; Jay 5; and Madison 29.

```
                                                      R Z
N T X X S L Y G A P X U Q J T U N     R W
O L S S B J Y Q B S U P Q Q I P O     O V
T C                             U S   E X
L T   T A N A S H Z P B J W     L I   Y T
I S   F R A N K L I N L A R     S D   P L
M E   Z T             F I     J A     D H
A I   Y E   T A V O N   H T   E M     Y C
H R   H B   S Y G V O   I I   T E     N T
O E   A O   S J   Z K   C N   D Q     L E
V S   C E   E Y   Y I   A G   X C     P K
L E   E H   R Q       G W   Z Y   X U
H O   D O   P H S Y A S S E   S A   Q X
Y E   Q G   M H Q M W T L E   S J   P A
T U   I X                 I T   P X
X V   J V C V E T L X X I I Q L   A G
Z A   D L X Q S T H X H Z F S D H   X Z
S T                             X Y   G
B G O P R I N T I N G U B O Q A Y K M N
Q Q Y R I F B G C I K X E Z X O T M C M
```

Find and circle the following nine words in the puzzle box.

WRITING PRINTING ESSAYS
SERIES HAMILTON MADISON
PRESS FRANKLIN JAY

The words may appear forward, backward, vertically, or diagonally.

Ben Franklin's Printing Press

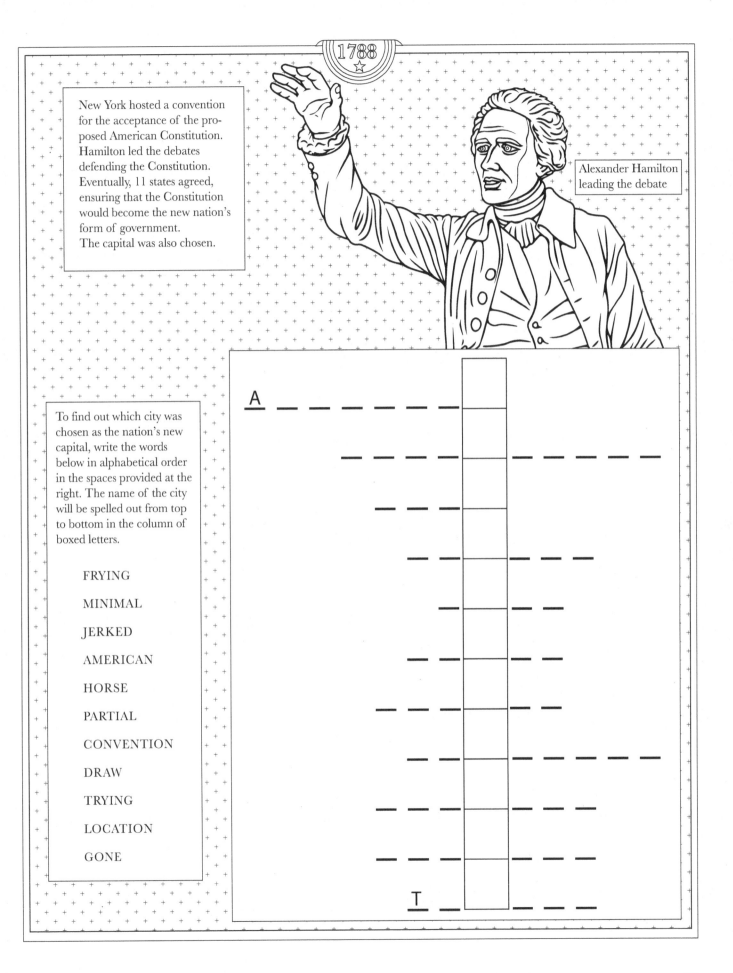

New York hosted a convention for the acceptance of the proposed American Constitution. Hamilton led the debates defending the Constitution. Eventually, 11 states agreed, ensuring that the Constitution would become the new nation's form of government.
The capital was also chosen.

Alexander Hamilton leading the debate

To find out which city was chosen as the nation's new capital, write the words below in alphabetical order in the spaces provided at the right. The name of the city will be spelled out from top to bottom in the column of boxed letters.

FRYING

MINIMAL

JERKED

AMERICAN

HORSE

PARTIAL

CONVENTION

DRAW

TRYING

LOCATION

GONE

A _ _ _ _ _ _ _ _

T _ _ _ _ _

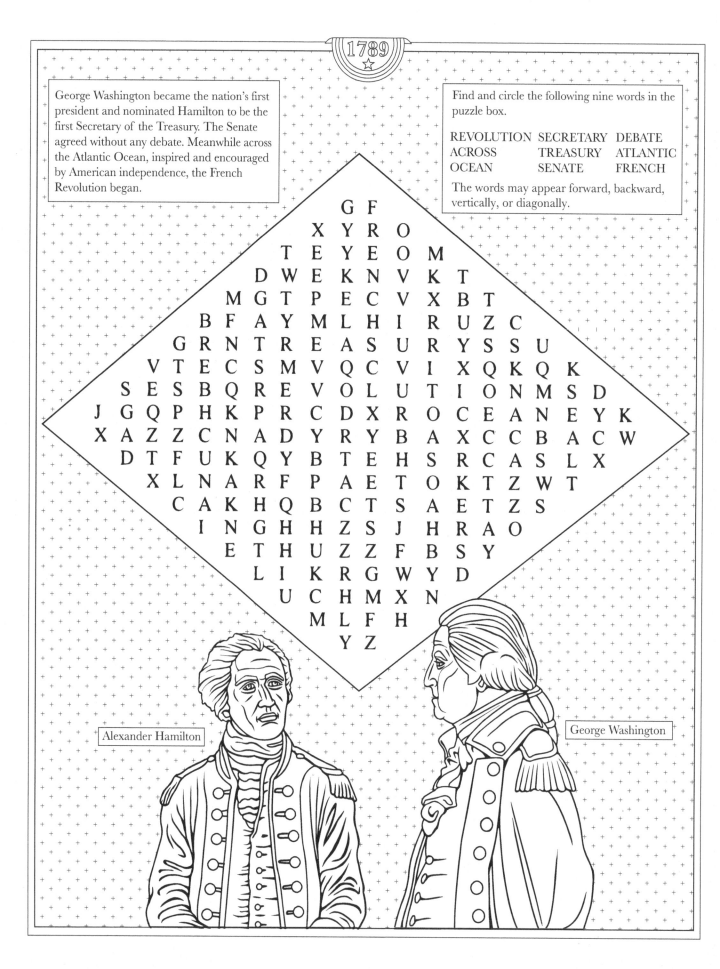

1789

George Washington became the nation's first president and nominated Hamilton to be the first Secretary of the Treasury. The Senate agreed without any debate. Meanwhile across the Atlantic Ocean, inspired and encouraged by American independence, the French Revolution began.

Find and circle the following nine words in the puzzle box.

REVOLUTION   SECRETARY   DEBATE
ACROSS   TREASURY   ATLANTIC
OCEAN   SENATE   FRENCH

The words may appear forward, backward, vertically, or diagonally.

Alexander Hamilton

George Washington

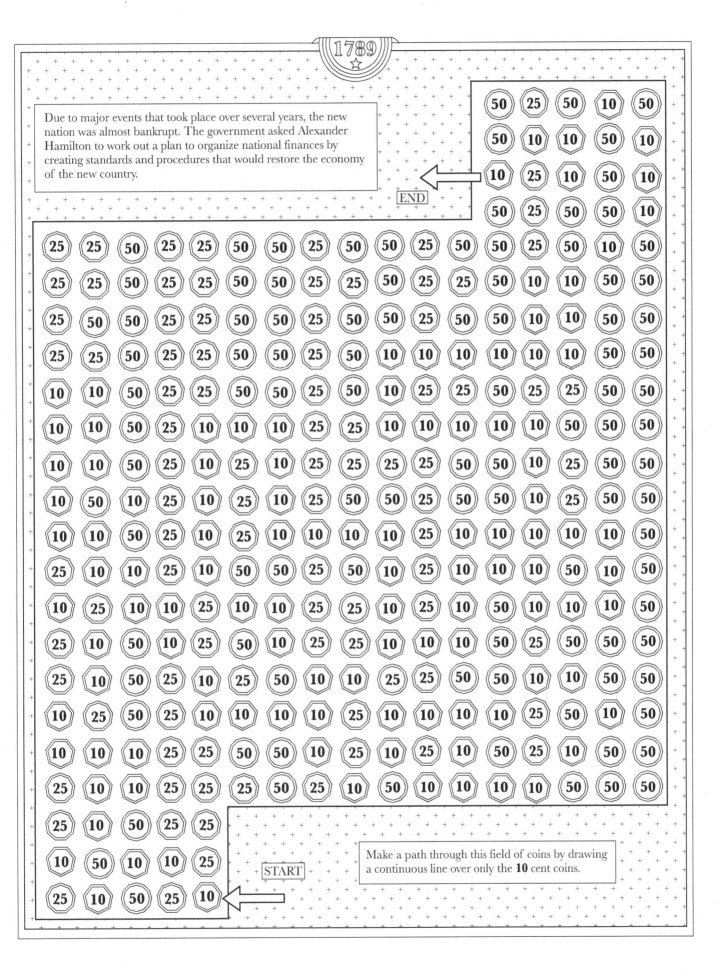

Due to major events that took place over several years, the new nation was almost bankrupt. The government asked Alexander Hamilton to work out a plan to organize national finances by creating standards and procedures that would restore the economy of the new country.

END

Make a path through this field of coins by drawing a continuous line over only the **10** cent coins.

START

At a dinner in the home of Secretary of State Thomas Jefferson, Alexander Hamilton and James Madison worked out an agreement that would eventually create a new national capital on the banks of the Potomac River.

WEESFTEB

		F		E	
7					

SEAKRTOUTYR

		S			K	
2						

FKREIDEHICNC

R				C		
	4		6		3	

NARAIGIHMIV

I		N		A	
	5				

PLIEPEPA

	P		I	

TADGOVELLEBIBSEE

	I		E			L	
						8	

PIUGDND

U		N	
1			

Mystery Food
1 2 3 4 5 6 7 8

Jefferson, Madison, and Hamilton

There are 16 foods listed below. Only seven are foods that would have been served in 1790. Unscramble the correct words and then write the letters of the numbered boxes into the bottom row to discover another food from the colonial era.

Beef Stew
Hamburgers
Roast Turkey
Tacos
Fried Chicken
French Fries
Hero Sandwich
Virginia Ham

Apple Pie
Pizza
Boiled Vegetables
Potato Chips
Sushi
Hot Dogs
Pudding
Peanut Butter

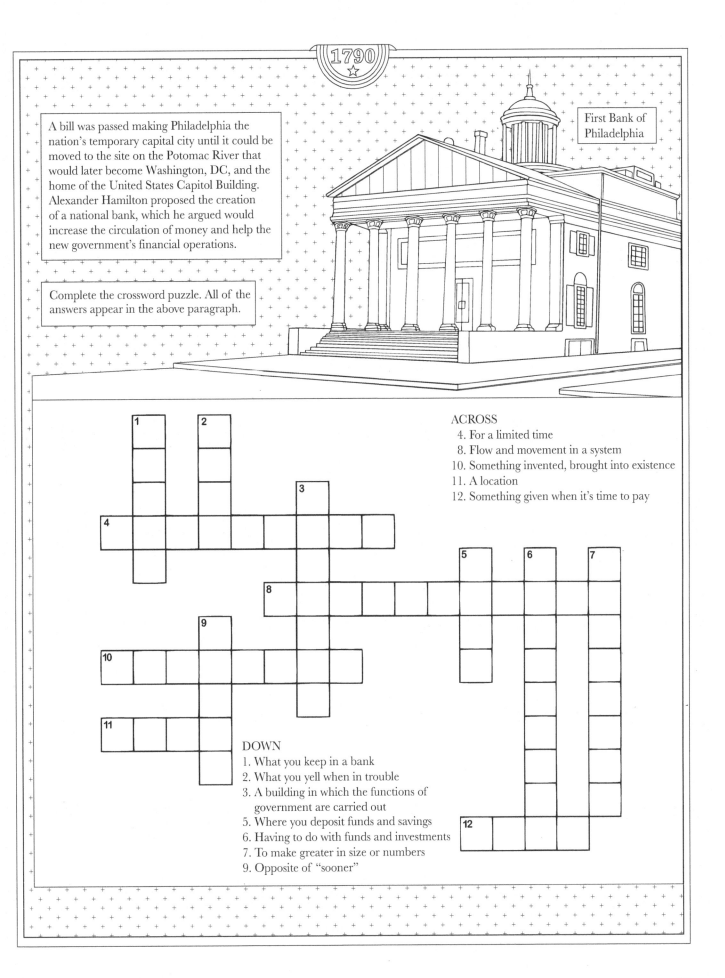

1790

A bill was passed making Philadelphia the nation's temporary capital city until it could be moved to the site on the Potomac River that would later become Washington, DC, and the home of the United States Capitol Building. Alexander Hamilton proposed the creation of a national bank, which he argued would increase the circulation of money and help the new government's financial operations.

First Bank of Philadelphia

Complete the crossword puzzle. All of the answers appear in the above paragraph.

ACROSS
4. For a limited time
8. Flow and movement in a system
10. Something invented, brought into existence
11. A location
12. Something given when it's time to pay

DOWN
1. What you keep in a bank
2. What you yell when in trouble
3. A building in which the functions of government are carried out
5. Where you deposit funds and savings
6. Having to do with funds and investments
7. To make greater in size or numbers
9. Opposite of "sooner"

27

1791

Despite strong opposition, President Washington signed Hamilton's national bank bill into law. Unhappy with this new direction, Thomas Jefferson and James Madison formed The Republicans, the new nation's first political party to oppose Washington's Federalist Party.

Form 10 words on each list from the letters that spell "Republican" and "Federalist."

REPUBLICAN	FEDERALIST

Thomas Jefferson

James Madison

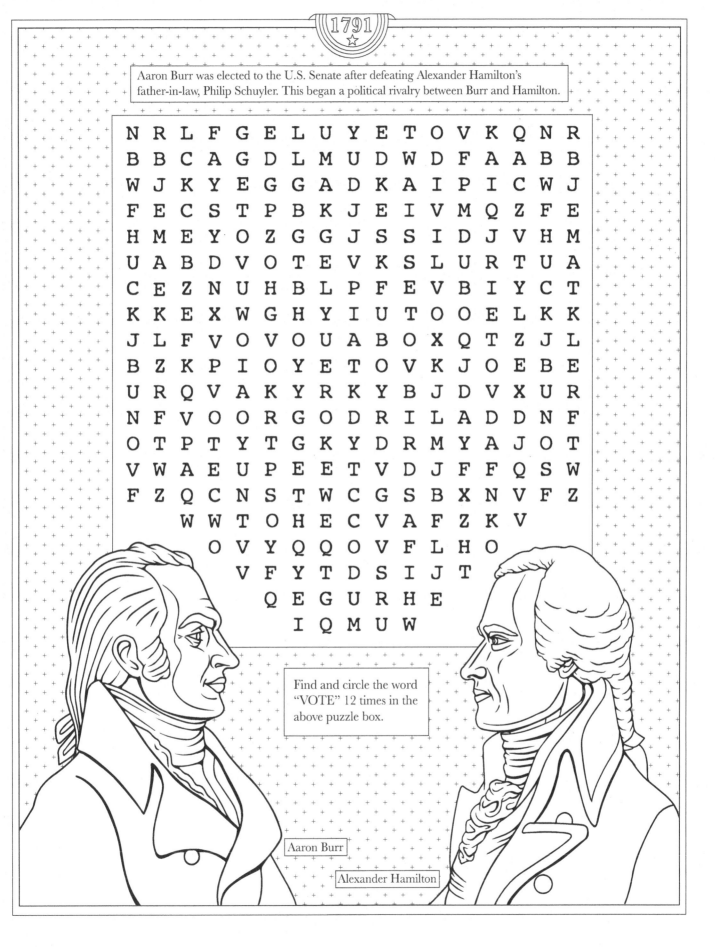

1791

Aaron Burr was elected to the U.S. Senate after defeating Alexander Hamilton's father-in-law, Philip Schuyler. This began a political rivalry between Burr and Hamilton.

```
N R L F G E L U Y E T O V K Q N R
B B C A G D L M U D W D F A A B B
W J K Y E G G A D K A I P I C W J
F E C S T P B K J E I V M Q Z F E
H M E Y O Z G G S S I D J V H M
U A B D V O T E V K S L U R T U A
C E Z N U H B L P F E V B I Y C T
K K E X W G H Y I U T O O E L K K
J L F V O V O U A B O X Q T Z J L
B Z K P I O Y E T O V K J O E B E
U R Q V A K Y R K Y B J D V X U R
N F V O O R G O D R I L A D D N F
O T P T Y T G K Y D R M Y A J O T
V W A E U P E E T V D J F F Q S W
F Z Q C N S T W C G S B X N V F Z
    W W T O H E C V A F Z K V
      O V Y Q Q O V F L H O
        V F Y T D S I J T
          Q E G U R H E
            I Q M U W
```

Find and circle the word "VOTE" 12 times in the above puzzle box.

Aaron Burr

Alexander Hamilton

29

Republicans accused Hamilton of improper financial dealings. Hamilton was convinced that Jefferson and Madison were trying to destroy him and upset the Union. These bitter political arguments headlined the country's newspapers and threatened to bring down Washington's presidency.

A	C	D	E	G	H	I	J	K	L	M	N	O	P	R	S	T	U	V	W	Y	Z
1	2	3	4	5	6	7	8	9	10	11	12	13	14	15	16	17	18	19	20	21	22

There were many newspapers in colonial times. Using the letter code above, write in the names of five newspapers of the era in the spaces provided.

Colonial Era Newsboy

5 15 4 4 12   11 13 18 12 17 1 7 12   14 1 17 15 7 13 17

1 11 4 15 7 2 1 12   1 14 13 10 10 13

12 4 20 14 13 15 17   6 4 15 1 10 3

15 1 10 4 7 5 6   11 7 12 4 15 19 1

9 4 12 17 18 2 9 21   5 1 22 4 17 17 4

Most residents, including President Washington and Alexander Hamilton, fled the city of Philadelphia after an outbreak of yellow fever began in the city. By the end of the epidemic thousands of people had died from the illness. Thomas Jefferson resigned as Secretary of State, and Hamilton became a more powerful person in President Washington's government.

Make your way through this city of Philadelphia maze from the Delaware River to the Schuylkill River.

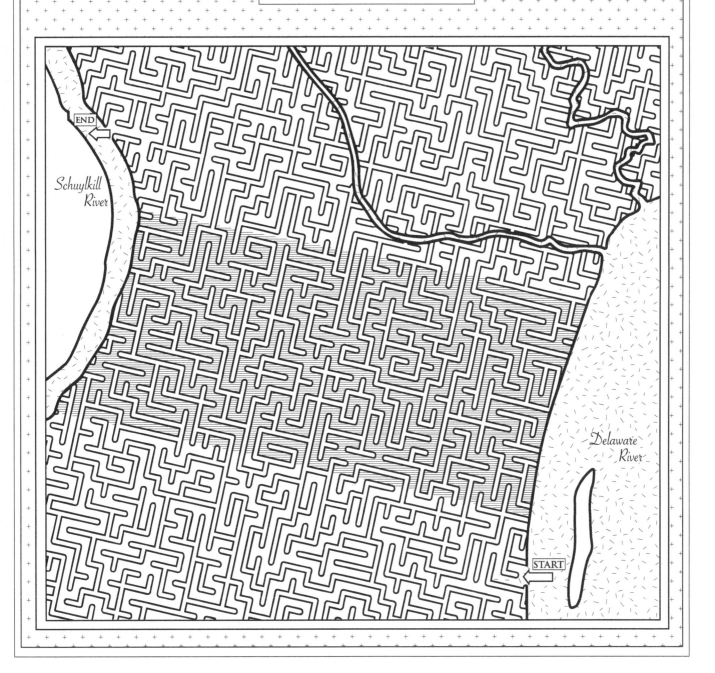

After imposing a federal tax on strong alcohol, Hamilton had to deal with what became known as the "Whiskey Rebellion." He and President Washington prepared to take military action, but the rebellion ended without much damage.

A	B	C	D	E	F	G	H	I	J	K	L	M

N	O	P	Q	R	S	T	U	V	W	X	Y	Z

Use the code above to find out where the rebellion took place.

Whiskey Rebellion Protesters

George Washington said farewell to the presidency and his vice president, John Adams, was elected the second president of the United States with 71 electoral votes over his opponent Thomas Jefferson's 68. At that time, the candidate with the most electoral votes became president, and the runner-up became vice president. Alexander Hamilton was not pleased with the outcome.

Find and circle the only two groupings that have this exact order of four stars and stripes boxes.

Alexander Hamilton

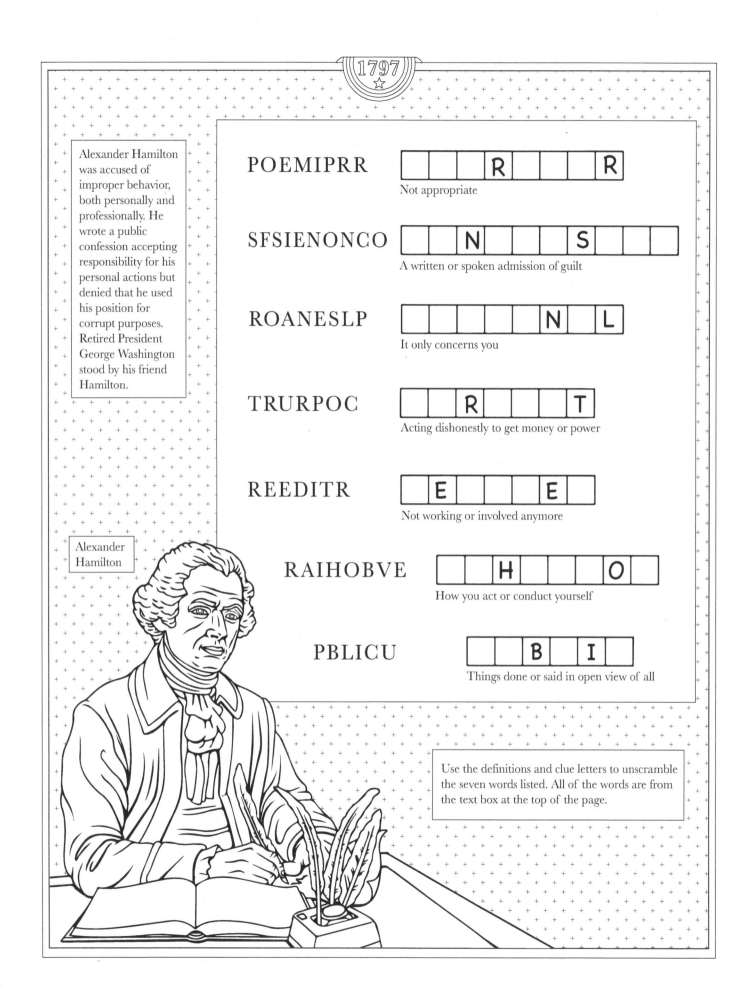

1797

Alexander Hamilton was accused of improper behavior, both personally and professionally. He wrote a public confession accepting responsibility for his personal actions but denied that he used his position for corrupt purposes. Retired President George Washington stood by his friend Hamilton.

Alexander Hamilton

POEMIPRR

| | | R | | | R |

Not appropriate

SFSIENONCO

| | N | | | S | | | |

A written or spoken admission of guilt

ROANESLP

| | | | | N | L |

It only concerns you

TRURPOC

| | R | | | T |

Acting dishonestly to get money or power

REEDITR

| E | | | E | | |

Not working or involved anymore

RAIHOBVE

| | H | | | O | |

How you act or conduct yourself

PBLICU

| | B | I | |

Things done or said in open view of all

Use the definitions and clue letters to unscramble the seven words listed. All of the words are from the text box at the top of the page.

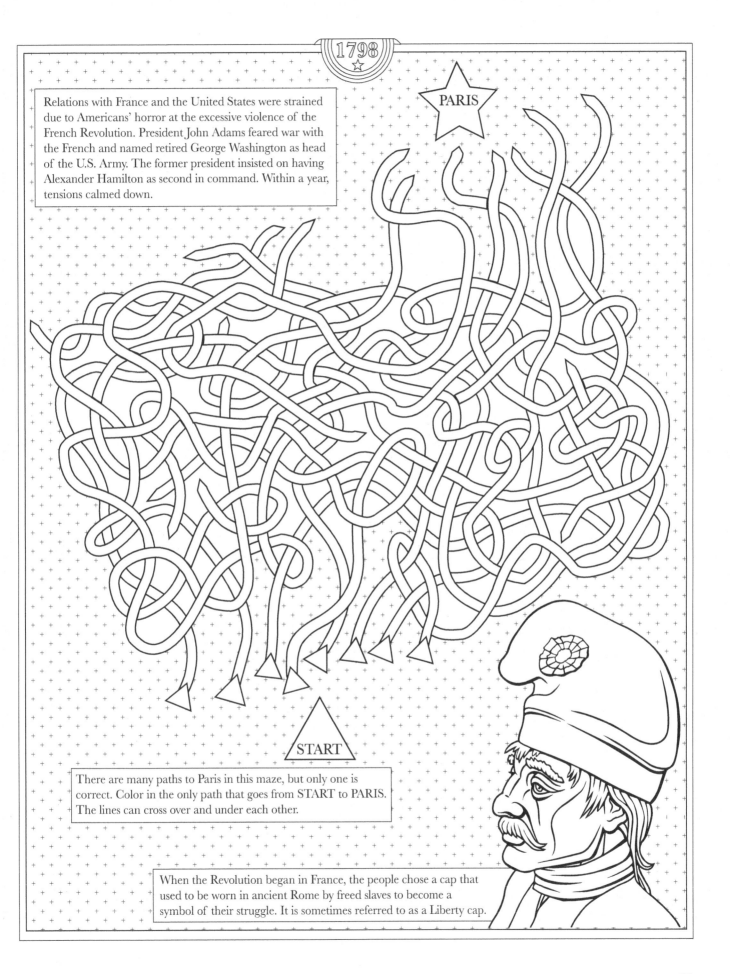

PARIS

Relations with France and the United States were strained due to Americans' horror at the excessive violence of the French Revolution. President John Adams feared war with the French and named retired George Washington as head of the U.S. Army. The former president insisted on having Alexander Hamilton as second in command. Within a year, tensions calmed down.

START

There are many paths to Paris in this maze, but only one is correct. Color in the only path that goes from START to PARIS. The lines can cross over and under each other.

When the Revolution began in France, the people chose a cap that used to be worn in ancient Rome by freed slaves to become a symbol of their struggle. It is sometimes referred to as a Liberty cap.

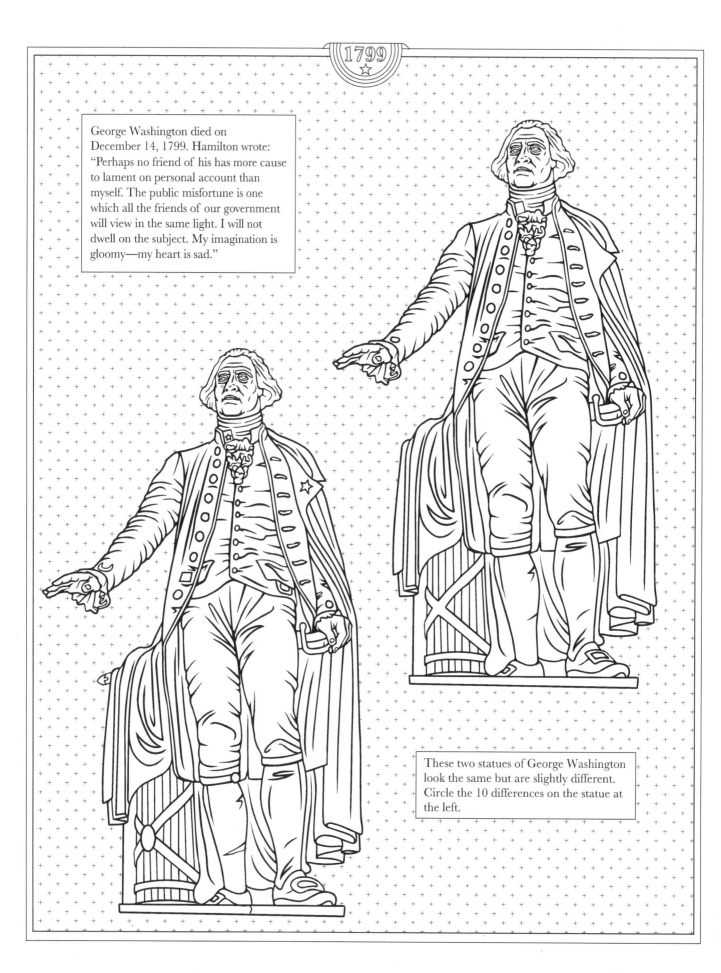

George Washington died on December 14, 1799. Hamilton wrote: "Perhaps no friend of his has more cause to lament on personal account than myself. The public misfortune is one which all the friends of our government will view in the same light. I will not dwell on the subject. My imagination is gloomy—my heart is sad."

These two statues of George Washington look the same but are slightly different. Circle the 10 differences on the statue at the left.

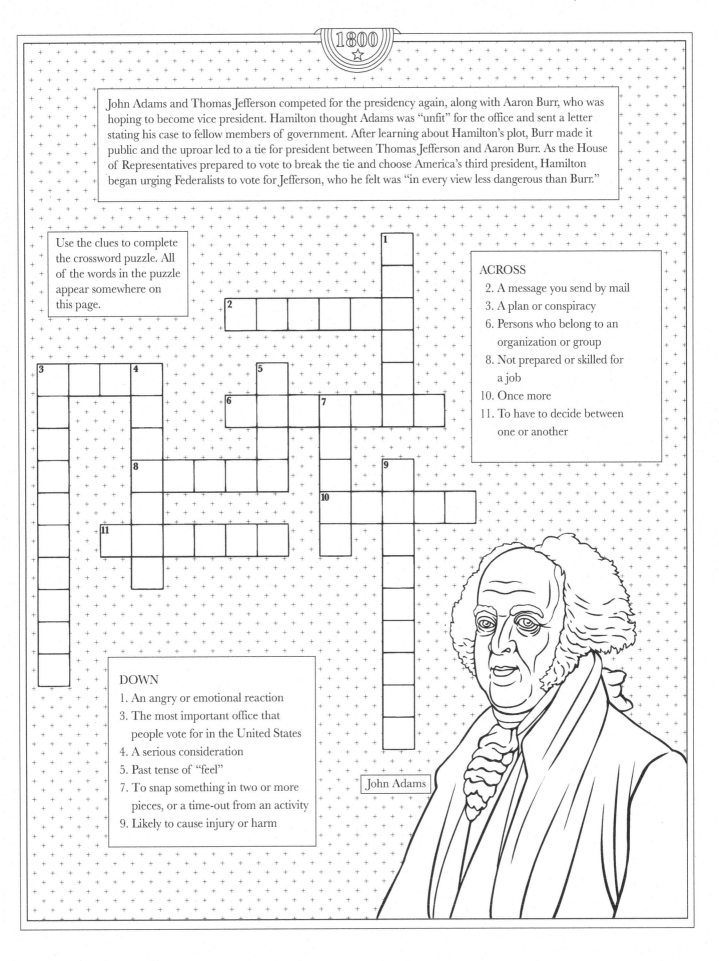

1800

John Adams and Thomas Jefferson competed for the presidency again, along with Aaron Burr, who was hoping to become vice president. Hamilton thought Adams was "unfit" for the office and sent a letter stating his case to fellow members of government. After learning about Hamilton's plot, Burr made it public and the uproar led to a tie for president between Thomas Jefferson and Aaron Burr. As the House of Representatives prepared to vote to break the tie and choose America's third president, Hamilton began urging Federalists to vote for Jefferson, who he felt was "in every view less dangerous than Burr."

Use the clues to complete the crossword puzzle. All of the words in the puzzle appear somewhere on this page.

ACROSS

2. A message you send by mail
3. A plan or conspiracy
6. Persons who belong to an organization or group
8. Not prepared or skilled for a job
10. Once more
11. To have to decide between one or another

DOWN

1. An angry or emotional reaction
3. The most important office that people vote for in the United States
4. A serious consideration
5. Past tense of "feel"
7. To snap something in two or more pieces, or a time-out from an activity
9. Likely to cause injury or harm

John Adams

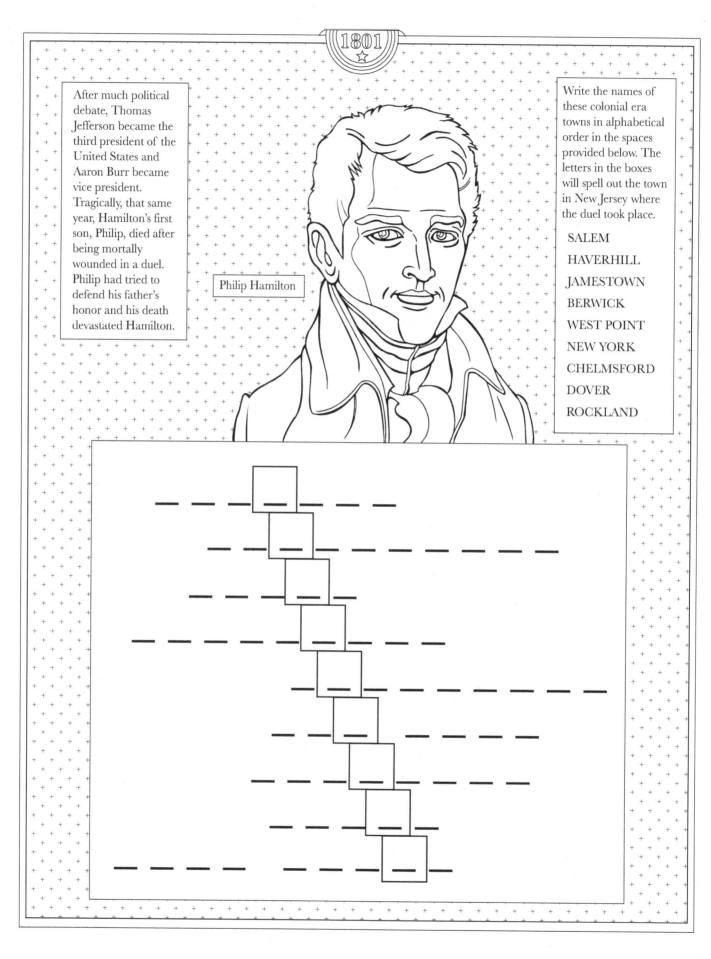

1801

After much political debate, Thomas Jefferson became the third president of the United States and Aaron Burr became vice president. Tragically, that same year, Hamilton's first son, Philip, died after being mortally wounded in a duel. Philip had tried to defend his father's honor and his death devastated Hamilton.

Philip Hamilton

Write the names of these colonial era towns in alphabetical order in the spaces provided below. The letters in the boxes will spell out the town in New Jersey where the duel took place.

SALEM

HAVERHILL

JAMESTOWN

BERWICK

WEST POINT

NEW YORK

CHELMSFORD

DOVER

ROCKLAND

1801

Hamilton, his wife, and eight children moved into a large home in upper Manhattan. It was the only home ever owned by Hamilton and remained in his family for 30 years after his death. He named the home after his grandfather's estate in Ayrshire, Scotland. Today it is part of the National Parks Service, which offers free tours.

There are nine alphabet grids with one letter missing. Write the missing letters in the corresponding numbered boxes below to find out what Hamilton named his home.

			1						2						3		

39

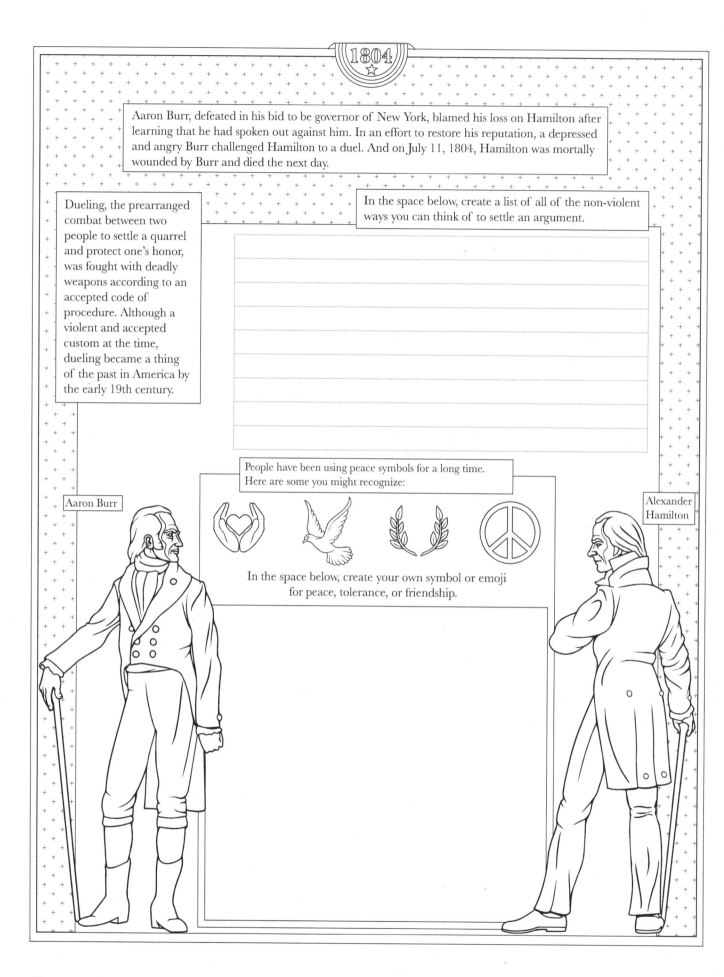

1804

Aaron Burr, defeated in his bid to be governor of New York, blamed his loss on Hamilton after learning that he had spoken out against him. In an effort to restore his reputation, a depressed and angry Burr challenged Hamilton to a duel. And on July 11, 1804, Hamilton was mortally wounded by Burr and died the next day.

Dueling, the prearranged combat between two people to settle a quarrel and protect one's honor, was fought with deadly weapons according to an accepted code of procedure. Although a violent and accepted custom at the time, dueling became a thing of the past in America by the early 19th century.

In the space below, create a list of all of the non-violent ways you can think of to settle an argument.

Aaron Burr

People have been using peace symbols for a long time. Here are some you might recognize:

In the space below, create your own symbol or emoji for peace, tolerance, or friendship.

Alexander Hamilton

40

ALEXANDER HAMILTON

Elizabeth Schuyler Hamilton died on November 9, 1854, at the age of 97. Despite her own financial difficulties after being widowed with seven children, she spent much of her life taking part in charitable activities. She was buried alongside her husband in the graveyard of Trinity Church in Manhattan.

Elizabeth Schuyler Hamilton

THE PATRIOT OF INCORRUPTIBLE INTEGRITY, THE SOLDIER OF APPROVED VALOUR, THE STATESMAN OF CONSUMMATE WISDOM, WHOSE TALENTS AND VIRTUES WILL BE ADMIRED BY GRATEFUL POSTERITY LONG AFTER THIS MARBLE SHALL HAVE MOULDERED INTO DUST.

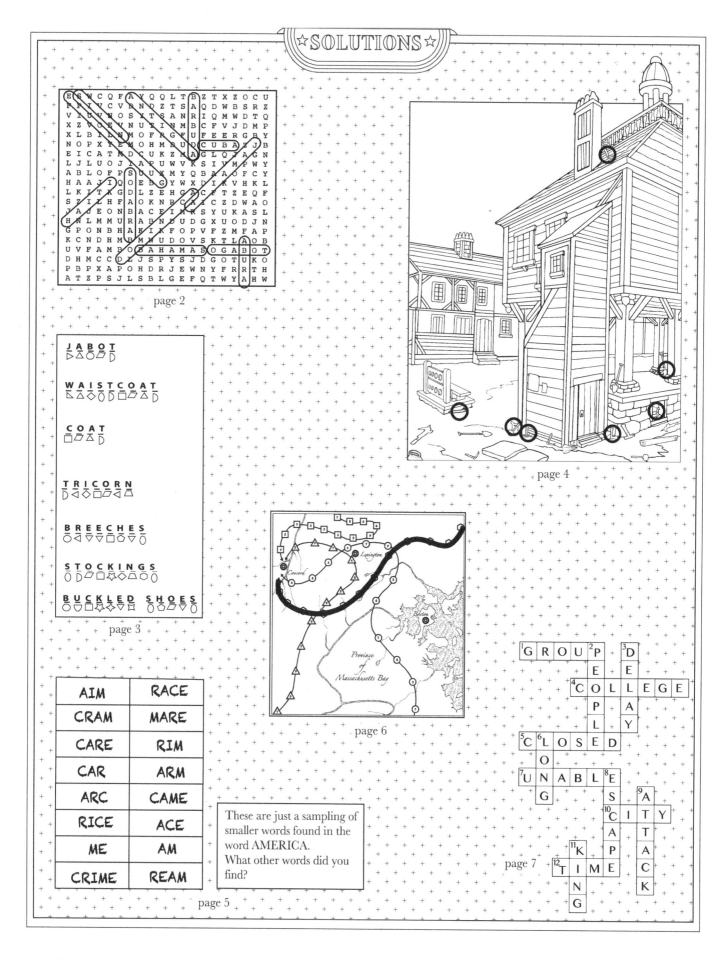

page 2

JABOT

WAISTCOAT

COAT

TRICORN

BREECHES

STOCKINGS

BUCKLED SHOES

page 3

page 4

page 6

AIM	RACE
CRAM	MARE
CARE	RIM
CAR	ARM
ARC	CAME
RICE	ACE
ME	AM
CRIME	REAM

These are just a sampling of smaller words found in the word AMERICA. What other words did you find?

page 5

page 7

¹GROUP ²P ³D
⁴COLLEGE
E A
P Y
L
⁵C⁶LOSED
O O
⁷UNABL⁸E ⁹A
¹⁰CITY
S T
¹¹K T
A¹²TIME A
C C
K

42

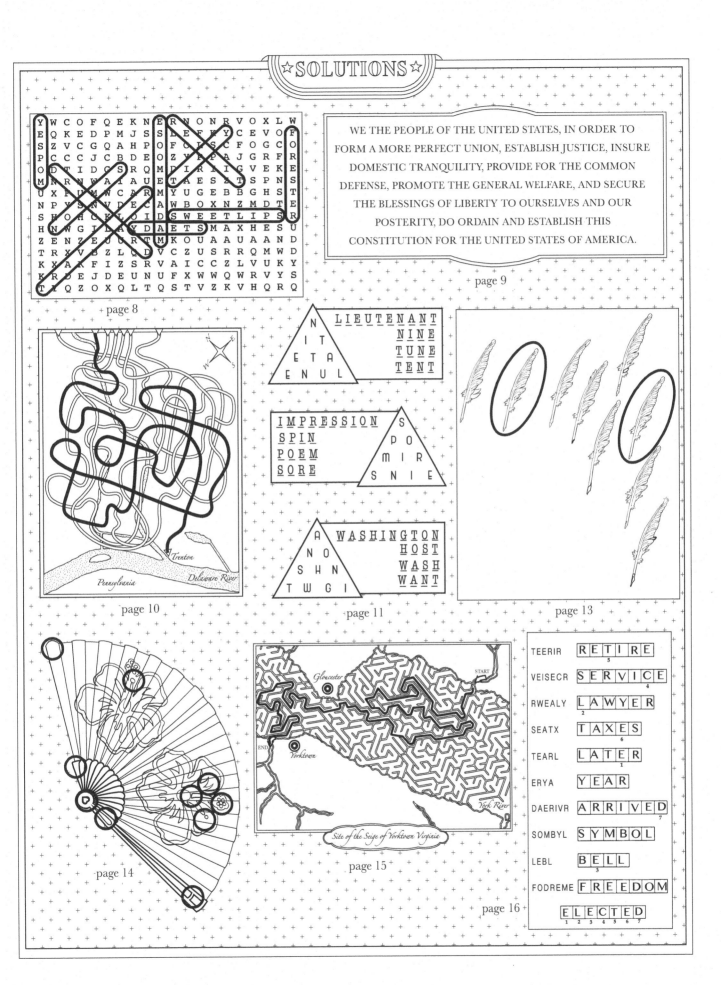

☆ SOLUTIONS ☆

page 8

WE THE PEOPLE OF THE UNITED STATES, IN ORDER TO FORM A MORE PERFECT UNION, ESTABLISH JUSTICE, INSURE DOMESTIC TRANQUILITY, PROVIDE FOR THE COMMON DEFENSE, PROMOTE THE GENERAL WELFARE, AND SECURE THE BLESSINGS OF LIBERTY TO OURSELVES AND OUR POSTERITY, DO ORDAIN AND ESTABLISH THIS CONSTITUTION FOR THE UNITED STATES OF AMERICA.

page 9

page 10

LIEUTENANT
NINE
TUNE
TENT

IMPRESSION
SPIN
POEM
SORE

WASHINGTON
HOST
WASH
WANT

page 11

page 13

page 14

Site of the Siege of Yorktown Virginia

page 15

TEERIR — RETIRE
VEISECR — SERVICE
RWEALY — LAWYER
SEATX — TAXES
TEARL — LATER
ERYA — YEAR
DAERIVR — ARRIVED
SOMBYL — SYMBOL
LEBL — BELL
FODREME — FREEDOM

ELECTED

page 16

43

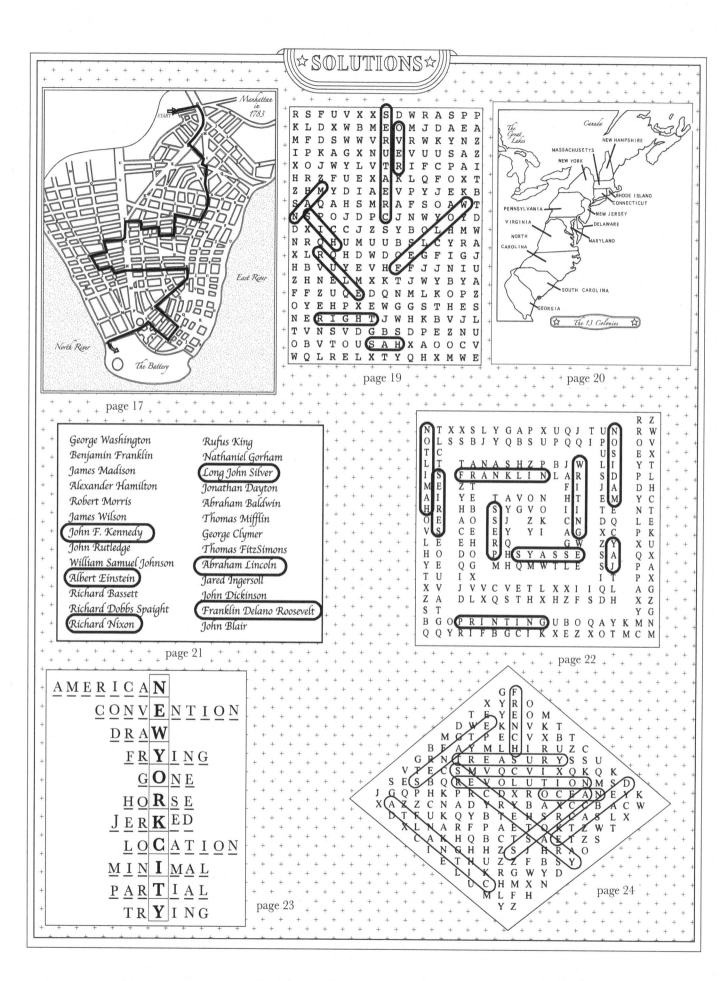

page 17

page 19

page 20

page 21

page 22

page 23

page 24

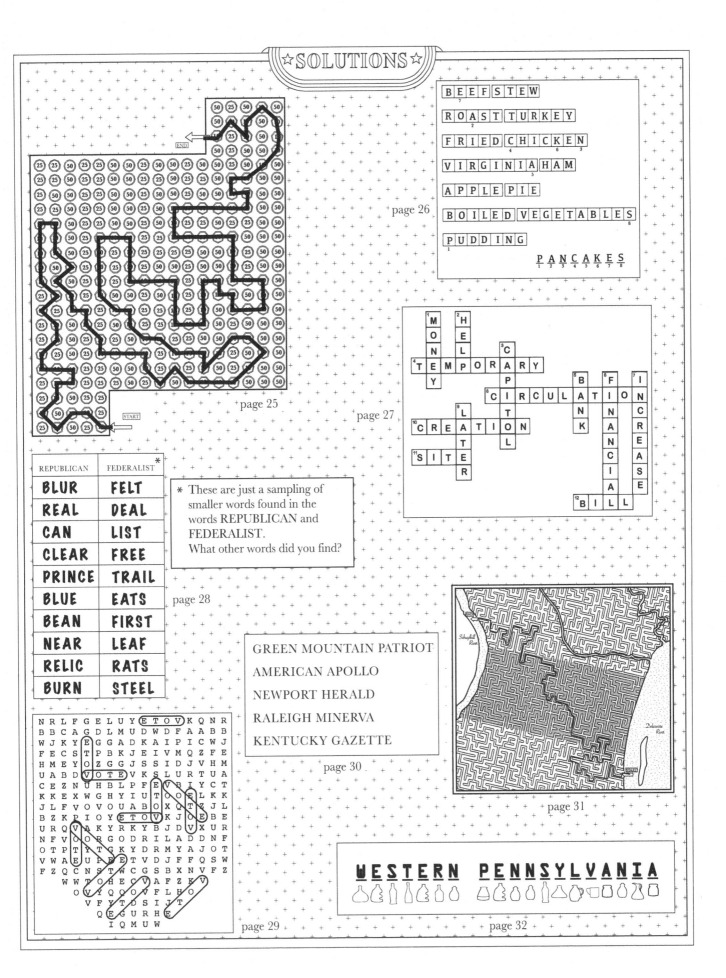

page 26

BEEFSTEW
ROASTTURKEY
FRIEDCHICKEN
VIRGINIAHAM
APPLEPIE
BOILEDVEGETABLES
PUDDING

PANCAKES

page 25

page 27

REPUBLICAN	FEDERALIST*
BLUR	FELT
REAL	DEAL
CAN	LIST
CLEAR	FREE
PRINCE	TRAIL
BLUE	EATS
BEAN	FIRST
NEAR	LEAF
RELIC	RATS
BURN	STEEL

* These are just a sampling of smaller words found in the words REPUBLICAN and FEDERALIST.
What other words did you find?

page 28

GREEN MOUNTAIN PATRIOT
AMERICAN APOLLO
NEWPORT HERALD
RALEIGH MINERVA
KENTUCKY GAZETTE

page 30

page 31

page 29

page 32

WESTERN PENNSYLVANIA

45

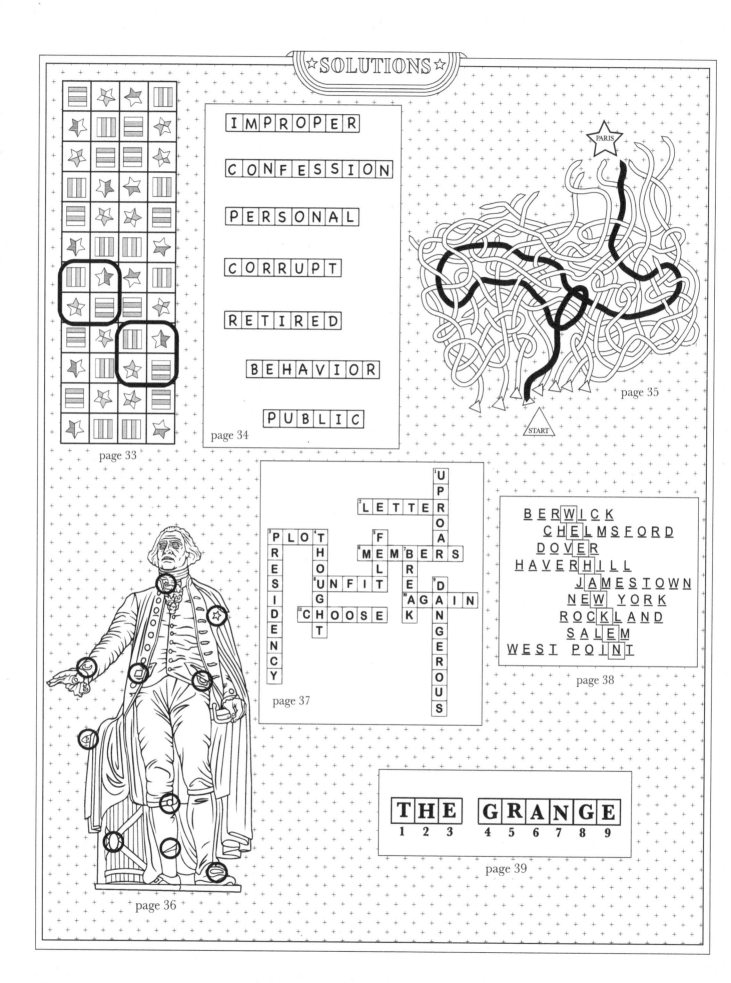

page 33

IMPROPER
CONFESSION
PERSONAL
CORRUPT
RETIRED
BEHAVIOR
PUBLIC

page 34

page 35

PARIS

START

page 37

¹U
²LETTER P
³P T ⁵F R
R H ⁶MEMBERS A
E O ⁴FELT E
S ⁸UNFIT K ⁹D
I G ¹⁰AGAIN A
D ¹¹CHOOSE K N
E T G
N E
C R
Y O
U
S

BERWICK
CHELMSFORD
DOVER
HAVERHILL
JAMESTOWN
NEW YORK
ROCKLAND
SALEM
WEST POINT

page 38

page 36

THE GRANGE
1 2 3 4 5 6 7 8 9

page 39

46